# Dogs to the Rescue

Some dogs can find and
rescue people.
They are called rescue dogs.

Some dogs can find and rescue people trapped in deep snow.

How do these dogs find people in the snow?

# DARING DOGS

## Contents

Alison Hawes

Story illustrated by
Ned Woodman

## Find out about

- How some dogs rescue people

## Tricky words

- rescue
- people
- trapped
- where
- mountains
- buildings

Introduce these tricky words and help the reader when they come across them later!

## Text starter

Some dogs can rescue people who are trapped in deep snow, lost on a mountain or trapped in a building. They show the rescue people where to search.

These dogs can smell where the people are trapped.

They show the rescue team where to dig.

Some dogs can find
and rescue people
lost on mountains.

These dogs can smell where the people have been.

They show the rescue team where to go.

Rescue dogs have a fantastic sense of smell!

Some dogs can find and rescue people trapped under buildings.

How do these dogs find the trapped people?

These dogs can smell where the people are trapped.

They show the rescue team where to dig.

Rescue dogs can help
lost people.

# Quiz

## Text Detective

- Why do rescue teams use dogs?
- Would you like to work in a rescue team with dogs?

## Word Detective

- Phonic Focus: Final letter sounds
  Page 5: Find a word that ends with 'g'.
- Page 4: Find a word that means 'stuck'.
- Page 7: Find the word 'show'.

## Super Speller

Read these words:

some    find    help

Now try to spell them!

HA! HA! HA!

**Q** Why did the dog sit near the fire?

**A** He wanted to be a hot dog!

11

# Before Reading

## In this story

 Tim

 The Pest

 Buster

## Tricky words

- wanted
- park
- hold
- lead
- pulled
- over

Introduce these tricky words and help the reader when they come across them later!

## Story starter

Tim lives with his mum and his little sister. His mum is always making him look after his sister. Tim calls her the Pest. One day, Tim took Gran's dog, Buster, to the park.

# Tim, the Pest
## and the
# Big Dog

Tim and Buster wanted to go to the park.
The Pest wanted to go too.

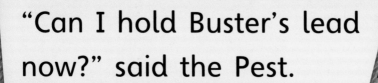

"Can I hold Buster's lead now?" said the Pest.

"No!" said Tim.
"Buster will pull you over."

Buster pulled and pulled on the lead.

He pulled Tim over!

Buster ran off.

He ran into the big pond.

He got mud all over him!

Tim ran over to the pond.
He got Buster's lead.

He pulled Buster over
to the Pest.

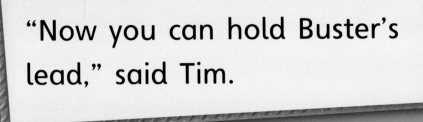

"Now you can hold Buster's lead," said Tim.

The Pest got mud all over her!

# Quiz

## Text Detective

- Where did Buster run to?
- Why did Tim let the Pest hold Buster's lead at the end of the story?

## Word Detective

- Phonic Focus: Final letter sounds
  Page 19: Find two words that end with 'd'.
- Page 13: Find a word that rhymes with 'shark'.
- Page 15: Find a word that means 'tugged'.

## Super Speller

Read these words:

had     pull     ran

Now try to spell them!

**Q** What do a dog and a tree have in common?

**A** Bark!

24